Mummie,

With Best Love and wishes for a
Happy Birthday and many more of
them,

from

Eleanor Mary Teresa

March 8th 1951

BRITAIN IN PICTURES
THE BRITISH PEOPLE IN PICTURES

BRITISH MOUNTAINEERS

GENERAL EDITOR
W. J. TURNER

The Editor is most grateful to all those who have
so kindly helped in the selection of illustrations
especially to officials of the various public
Museums Libraries and Galleries and
to all others who have generously
allowed pictures and MSS
to be reproduced

BRITISH
MOUNTAINEERS

F. S. SMYTHE

WITH
8 PLATES IN COLOUR
AND
22 ILLUSTRATIONS IN
BLACK & WHITE

COLLINS · 14 ST. JAMES'S PLACE · LONDON
MCMXLVI

PRODUCED BY
ADPRINT LIMITED LONDON

FIRST PUBLISHED 1942
SECOND IMPRESSION 1946

PRINTED IN GREAT BRITAIN BY
CLARKE & SHERWELL LTD NORTHAMPTON
ON MELLOTEX BOOK PAPER MADE BY
TULLIS RUSSELL & CO LTD MARKINCH SCOTLAND

LIST OF ILLUSTRATIONS

PLATES IN COLOUR

BLACK AND WHITE ILLUSTRATIONS

SHORT BIBLIOGRAPHY

Scrambles Amongst the Alps
   By Edward Whymper

The Playground of Europe
   By Sir Leslie Stephen

Everest 1933
   By Hugh Rutledge

My Climbs in the Alps and Caucasus
   By A. F. Mummery

On High Hills
   By G. Winthrop Young

The Mountain Way—an Anthology
   By R. L. G. Irving

EDITORIAL NOTE

The chapter 'A Personal Adventure' is included at the special request
of the Editor as it gives those who are not themselves mountaineers—
and they will be the majority of the readers of this book—a vivid account
at first hand of a climber's actual experience

THE CLUB ROOM AT ZERMATT IN 1864
Engraving by Edward Whymper from *Scrambles Amongst the Alps*, 1871

THE PIONEERS

NOWADAYS, mountain climbing is considered one of the world's most adventurous sports. It is both a stimulus and a test, a stimulus in that it enables men and women leading sedentary lives in cities, offices and factories to rejuvenate themselves through hard exercise in health-giving sun and air, a test because it brings out qualities of determination, leadership, strength, skill and endurance. Then, it brings its devotees into contact with Nature untamed and unspoiled, Nature at her grandest and most beautiful. It appeals particularly to Englishmen, who throughout the ages have inherited a love of adventure and the pioneering instinct that makes its accomplishment possible.

From the earliest times, mountains have been regarded as mysterious and aloof from the ordinary affairs of plain and city. Our ancestors looked upon them with awe and fear. Gods, devils, dragons, the spirits of the damned dwelt on their inaccessible summits ready to wreak vengeance on the rash intruder. They refused the plough, interposed barriers between peoples ; they were of no commercial value ; they were ugly.

Yet, as man slowly and painfully emancipated himself from his primeval fears and superstitions, a spirit of inquiry gained ascendancy. What was to be found on those terrible summits where the lightning played and the blizzard had its lair ? What did the world look like from icy heights where the clouds paused to repose themselves ? Every age has produced men ahead of their time in thought and deed ; poets, philosophers, scholars, scientists

7

and explorers. So it was in mountaineering. Fearfully and cautiously, then with a greater daring, familiarity and understanding, a few bold spirits began to cross mountain ranges and climb mountains. At first this was usually for the sake of commercial enterprise or for military reasons. The Alpine passes were opened up for both purposes, from the time when Hannibal drove his elephants across them to the time when immense tunnels were driven to link Italy with France and Switzerland. Slowly the spirit of inquiry overcame a repugnance for mountains as useless, ugly and inconvenient excrescences and it began to be realised that they were beautiful also, and that to view them and adventure upon them was an inspiring experience. Religious considerations had something to do with this. Since Moses ascended Mount Sinai to receive the Ten Commandments, down to the present day, most of the world's religions have associated mountains with their mysticism, and this provoked a pantheism which has helped to influence man's feelings for the heights.

Englishmen were not only pioneers in the sport of mountaineering but they took a great part in the opening up of difficult mountainous countries. To them was due the crossing and exploration of the Rockies, settlements in the mountainous areas of New Zealand, the exploration of the Himalayas and many other regions. As with the sea and, more recently, the air, the mountains were in their blood. It is true that the spirit of adventure, and it must be added a zest for commerce, were greater in the first place than a liking for mountains ; Dr. Johnson's opinion of the Scottish Highlands was that "this uniformity of barrenness can afford very little amusement to the traveller." In Goldsmith's view, hills "interrupt every prospect." Two typical views were those of John Evelyn, the diarist, for whom the Simplon Pass consisted of "horrid and fearful craggs and tracts" ; and of Bishop Berkeley who, on the Mont Cenis Pass, was "put out of humour by the most horrible precipices," and considered that "every object that here presents itself is excessively miserable." It was left to poets such as Byron, Words-worth and Shelley to perceive beauty in mountains, and to a few mountain-lovers such as Bourrit, Conrad Gesner, Simler and an enterprising Catholic priest, Father Placidus à Spescha, to want to climb mountains for their own sake as well as merely to view them.

In the eighteenth century, when the grand tour of Europe was becoming popular as an itinerary to be undertaken by every young man of wealth, erudition, and fashion, Chamonix was visited by an active young Englishman named Robert Windham together with his tutor, Dr. Pococke, and sundry of his friends. They engaged some guides and porters and scaled the steep pine forests to the Montanvert. Not content with this they ventured upon the Mer de Glace and were thus in all probability the first Englishmen to tread an Alpine glacier.

Forty-five years later, in 1786, Mont Blanc was scaled by Dr. Paccard and a chamois hunter Jacques Balmat, largely as a result of the enthusiasm

VIEW OF MONT FURKA WITH THE RHÔNE GLACIER
Water colour by William Pars, c.1770

THE LÜTSCHINEN ISSUING FROM THE LOWER GRINDELWALD GLACIER

Coloured aquatint by C. M. Descourtis after G. Wolf

of that great scientist De Saussure who, as early as 1760, considered that the mountain ought to be climbed, and subsequently offered a reward to anyone who could find a way to the summit. De Saussure himself scaled the mountain the following year, and was followed about a week later by Colonel Mark Beaufoy of the Tower Hamlets Militia. This last was the first great British ascent in the Alps and it was followed next year by that of Mr. Woodley : he was accompanied by Bourrit and a Dutchman named Camper, but was the sole member of the party to reach the summit.

After that, the ascent of Mont Blanc became something of a fashionable adventure, whilst ascents began to be made elsewhere in the Alps. Such ascents were largely exploratory and the majority of them were made for scientific reasons, as the time had not yet arrived when it was considered justifiable to climb mountains save in the cause of science. There were of course exceptions. The two summits of the Gross Glockner, the highest mountain in Austria, were scaled in 1799 and 1800 respectively by an Austrian party animated primarily by enthusiasm for the mountain, whilst there were numerous other ascents of an exploratory rather than scientific nature. On the whole, however, the opening up of the easier snow summits of the Alps had a scientific background and is associated with names such as Agassiz, Desor, De Saussure and Professor Forbes. The last named was a Scotsman, and although his interests were primarily scientific and he specialised in the study of glaciers, he was undoubtedly a mountaineer with a genuine love of mountains. He made various ascents including those of the Jungfrau and Riffelhorn, both of which mountains, however, had already been climbed. Of the latter peak an interesting story remains to be told. It was generally assumed to have been first climbed in 1841 by a party of English students. Thirty-three years later, some American tourists on the summit were engaged in the fascinating pastime of dislodging boulders and hurling them down the precipice on to the glacier below when they came upon a javelin or spear head. It would seem, therefore, that even if mountains were regarded with abhorrence throughout the Middle Ages there were times when primitive man ventured upon their summits.

After Forbes came John Ball, an indefatigable traveller and mountaineer who did much to popularise the Alps by compiling an Alpine guide-book ; he was Colonial Under-Secretary in Lord Palmerston's Administration. Another Englishman who drew public attention to the Alps, but in another way, was Albert Smith. He was a prototype of the young hiker, camper and mountaineer of to-day who, with limited means, spends a short but infinitely precious holiday in the hills. Thus far mountaineering had been, and was to be for many years, the almost exclusive preserve of eclectics, of Government officials, University dons and professional men generally, who with ample time and money at their disposal could afford long holidays in the Alps and the expense of guides. In 1838, Smith, then twenty-two years old, arrived at Chamonix with twelve pounds in his pocket. Instantly he fell under the spell of the mountains and was so anxious to make the ascent of Mont Blanc that he offered to go as porter for anyone who would take him. He failed in his ambition, but returned to the attack in 1851 with some Oxford undergraduates who were delighted to climb with him when they learned that he was "Mr. Smith of London, the well-known comic author." This time he succeeded, but the ascent provoked much undesirable publicity. In the course of an article, the *Daily News* wrote, "De Saussure's observations and reflections on Mont Blanc live in his poetical philosophy ; those of Mr. Albert Smith will be most appropriately recorded in a tissue of indifferent puns and stale fast witticisms, with an incessant straining after smartness. The aimless scramble of the four pedestrians to the top of Mont Blanc . . . will not go far to redeem the somewhat equivocal reputation of the herd of English tourists in Switzerland for a mindless and rather vulgar redundance of animal spirits."

But Albert Smith remained unabashed. He was by nature a born showman, and such are impervious to criticism and abuse. He wrote an interesting and entertaining book about Mont Blanc and, constructing a model of the mountain, set out to describe it and his experiences to all and sundry. His *Mont Blanc in a Box* show was a popular success and, however much it may have been scorned by the eclectics, undoubtedly did much to bring the beauty and interest of the Alps to the public attention.

"PER NIVES SEMPITERNAS RUPESQUE TREMENDAS"
Engraving from *Peaks, Passes and Glaciers*,
Volume I, edited by John Ball, 1859

THE GOLDEN AGE

IT is not improbable that Albert Smith's popular Alpine entertainment had something to do with the development of the sport of mountaineering, as distinct from the scientific-cum-exploration and dare-devil adventure attitude that prevailed from 1786 almost to the middle of the nineteenth century. Edward Whymper, who was later to write the most dramatic of all chapters in the history of the sport, recorded in his diary that he witnessed it as a youth, and so too must many others of the pioneers. Albert Smith's enthusiasm was too great and his showmanship too expert not to leave a mark.

Precisely how or why mountaineering took on a new lease of life as a pure sport is not easy to say. It is generally assumed that Mr. Justice Wills's ascent of the Wetterhorn in 1854 ushered it in in this guise. Dates, however, are apt to be misleading, and while this ascent undoubtedly helped to set a new fashion, its importance has been over-estimated. Furthermore, this ascent, still assumed by many to have been the first of that mountain, was actually only the fourth. It did, however, mark the beginning of an epoch, for the ensuing ten years saw the conquest of practically all the great peaks of the Alps. These conquests were almost all of them made by Englishmen and their guides, and it was they who developed the craft, the technique and the skill necessary to overcome peaks far more difficult than any hitherto assailed ; they who by persuasion and example raised from rude Alpine peasantry a *corps d'élite* of guides, and improved the former rough-and-ready implements of mountaineering to suit the new and more exacting conditions of mountain craft. In a word, Englishmen were responsible for the great sport of mountaineering.

I have written of this sport that it was a new fashion. So it was, in a limited sense, but never had the followers of any fashion, not even those who sought notoriety by descending Niagara in barrels, to endure such obloquy as the dons, schoolmasters and parsons who set out to scale the untrodden peaks of the Alps. The revolution, for revolution it was, must be examined against the tendencies of the age. It was an age of peace but never of stagnation, an age in which the arts and sciences flourished apace, an age which had the potentialities for setting in motion something far better than the wheels of a materialism, which for the past half-century have raised dust clouds to choke and obscure the spiritual vision of man. It was as though some vision had been dimly discerned : the vision of the mountains ; and, lo, they were beautiful ; and more than being beautiful, they inspired a contest of a new nature, a friendly contest that had in it no jarring element, no bloodlust, that exercised every muscle, that lit every corner of the mind with beauty, that made for enduring friendships. All these things the pioneers perceived in mountain climbing and much else besides. They were content to have discovered something that was not merely new, a phase, a fashion, but something enduring like the snowy heights that would provide enjoyment and inspiration for generations unborn. Mountains were no longer ugly and terrifying. An aspect of Nature had been discovered, or re-discovered, it matters not which ; the adventurous instinct of Englishmen had found a new outlet, something to off-set the steady days of peace and prosperity. The ascent of the Wetterhorn signposted a way already visible.

In his book, *Wanderings Among the High Alps*, Wills gives a dramatic account of the ascent :

"Suddenly, a startling cry of surprise and triumph rang through the air. A great block of ice bounded from the top of the parapet, and before it had well lighted on the glacier, Lauener exclaimed, 'Ich schaue den blauen himmel !' (I see blue sky). A thrill of astonishment and delight ran through our frames. Our enterprise had succeeded ! We were almost upon the actual summit. That wave above us, frozen, as it seemed, in the act of falling over ! Lauener's blows flew with redoubled energy. In a few minutes a practicable breach was made, through which he disappeared. . . . As I took the last step, Balmat disappeared from my sight ; my left shoulder grazed against the angle of the icy embrasure, while, on the right, the glacier fell abruptly away beneath me, towards an unknown and awful abyss ; a hand from an invisible person grasped mine ; I stepped across, and had passed the ridge of the Wetterhorn !"

Such accounts did much to instil enthusiasm in the minds of adventurous young Englishmen.

The great snow peaks were the first to be ascended, for they were the easiest to climb, and the art of rock climbing was not developed until the advent of the English. Thus the several peaks of Monte Rosa fell over a period of thirty-eight years. Dr. Parrot, a Russian, who made the first ascent of Ararat, scaled the Parrot Spitze (14,643 feet) in 1817, but it was not until 1855 that the highest and rockiest point of the mountain (15,217 feet) was ascended by five Englishmen, the brothers G. and C. Smyth, the Rev. Charles Hudson, Birkbeck and Stephenson.

While Albert Smith was busy lecturing and, incidentally, amassing a fortune of thirty thousand pounds, a growing band of young Englishmen were engaged in tackling the more difficult among the great Alpine peaks. Apart from those already mentioned, were E. S. Kennedy, T. W. Hinchliff, William and B. St. J. Mathews, F. Vaughan Hawkins, William Longman,

PROFESSOR J. D. FORBES AND E. S. KENNEDY
Engravings by H. G. Willink and Edward Whymper

the Rev. J. Llewellyn Davies, the Rev. J. F. Hardy and several others.
Many of them were accustomed to meet at one or other of the Alpine
centres such as Zermatt, Grindelwald and Chamonix, and on their return
home liked to discuss their experiences and make new plans for the future.
It was in this way that the first of all mountaineering clubs, the Alpine Club,
came to be formed in 1854. The first President was Kennedy, and there
certainly was never a more active or enterprising club, for it was between
1854 and 1865 that its members climbed the great majority of the more
difficult peaks of the Alps. At first the members met in Hinchliff's rooms
but the club presently acquired premises of its own, together with an indefatigable editor in John Ball, who collected the narratives of members
into the first of a series of books known to climbers the world over as *Peaks,
Passes, and Glaciers*. A little later, a club publication, *The Alpine Journal*,
was regularly produced, by means of which knowledge of mountains and
mountaineering, together with kindred arts and sciences, was disseminated.

In Britain, at least, the surest method of arousing enthusiasm in a new
sport is the formation of an enterprising club. It was not long before the
Alpine Club attracted members—men such as Professor John Tyndall, a
noted scientist of the Victorian era ; Sir Leslie Stephen, the foremost
literary critic of his time, and many others, including a young wood-
engraver named Edward Whymper. It is also interesting to note that Albert
Smith was an original member, and this in a club in which professional
qualifications, as well as purely mountaineering qualifications, were by no
means overlooked.

For many years mountaineering, as already indicated, appealed for the
most part to the leisured and professional classes. Every season little coteries
of climbers were to be found at Zermatt, Grindelwald and other centres.

Guides were employed, not because the climbers were necessarily incompetent to climb without them, but because the rigid Victorian standards of "gentlemanliness" demanded that the hard manual labour of load-carrying and step-cutting should be undertaken by professionals. At the same time, there were many guides who were something more than carriers and pointers-out of paths, men who readily learned to recognise practicable routes and who, by virtue of lifelong residence among mountains, grew to be expert craftsmen in the art of mountaineering. The rough, uncouth peasant soon became expert in the new technique, and trust, confidence and affection were established between him and his employer. Nowadays, when guiding as a business is rapidly becoming extinct, it is customary for some to sneer at the pioneers and to attribute their successes to the work of their guides. Such, however, was by no means the case. More often than not, the amateur was responsible, not only for the attempt on a new peak, but for the discovery of the route, and the guide's work was limited to step-cutting and leading up rocks.

The tourist who nowadays engages guides to climb the Matterhorn is shepherded up and down that mountain. The guide, who knows every foot of the way, is virtually master of the situation. In the Golden Age of mountaineering the amateur was ultimately responsible for all vital decisions.

Yet it was not to be supposed that the adventurous and independent spirit responsible for the development of this new sport of mountaineering should always be content to seek professional help. Many mountaineers are agreed that the most enterprising and brilliant climber of his time was the Rev. Charles Hudson who, as already noted, was associated with the Smyth brothers in the first ascent of the highest point of Monte Rosa. In 1853, at the age of twenty-five, he made, in defiance of all orthodox procedure, repeated attempts in the month of March to climb the Aiguille du Goûter of Mont Blanc, finally ascending alone almost to the summit and reconnoitring a new route up Mont Blanc. Two years later, he made guideless ascents of the Klein Matterhorn and the Breithorn, then, returning to the Chamonix district with his friends Ainslie, Kennedy and the Smyths, made the first guideless ascent of Mont Blanc, and at the same time opened up a new route to the summit from St. Gervais. During the next ten years he made a number of other first-rate ascents, including the first ascent of Mont Blanc over the Bosses du Dromédaire, the route now followed in preference to the Ancien Passage, the first complete passage of the Mönchjoch in the Bernese Oberland and the second ascent of the Aiguille Verte by a new route. Not only was he a self-reliant and skilful climber, but an expert route-finder into the bargain, with the eye for mountain topography of a born mountaineer. Thus, unlike Edward Whymper, who by the end of 1864 had made seven attempts to climb the Matterhorn, he was quick to seize upon the east face of that mountain as the most practicable route to the

MR. ALBERT SMITH'S 'ASCENT OF MONT BLANC'
The Egyptian Hall, Piccadilly, December, 1852

summit. His association with Whymper in the ultimate conquest of the peak, and his tragic death during the descent, will be told in the next chapter. In the public eye, Whymper more than anyone was the conqueror of the Matterhorn, but the fact is that Hudson's share in that conquest was in some respects greater than Whymper's; had he lived, he would have gone down to mountaineering posterity as the mountaineer *par excellence* of the Golden Age.

To mention all the British climbers of the 'fifties and 'sixties would be to catalogue a long list of names, but there are certain figures which cannot be omitted even from this brief account. Foremost among scientist-mountaineers was Professor Tyndall. As with Professor Forbes, science came first, but science was also a convenient peg on which to hang a love of mountain adventure, and his first ascent of the Zermatt Weisshorn and attempts on the Matterhorn were sporting ascents in which science, however much the mutations of the air, the structure of the glaciers and rocks, and the "atmospheric thrust" may have occupied his attention, was relegated to a relatively unimportant place. Then there was Professor Bonney, another scientist, who made many pioneer ascents, and crossed innumerable passes particularly in the then little-known French Alps; John Ball, who, as already mentioned, contributed much to a topographical knowledge of the Alps, in particular the Eastern Alps and Dolomites, and the "irrepressible" F. F. Tuckett whose expeditions occupy no less than fifteen pages in the Alpine Club register ; indeed this great mountaineer and traveller really deserves a book to himself. Then there were the Walker brothers, the Birkbecks, the Rev. H. B. George, F. C. Grove, E. S. Kennedy who made a number of fine guideless expeditions, the three Mathews brothers, A. W. Moore, A. M. W. Adams Reilly who made many fine ascents in the course of his surveys, and numerous others.

After *Scrambles Amongst the Alps*, by Edward Whymper, a book which was later to attract universal attention and inspire countless young men to climb mountains, the most attractive volume dealing with ascents in the Golden Age is *The Playground of Europe*, by Sir Leslie Stephen. This "fleetest of foot of the Alpine Brotherhood" brought a critical and discerning eye to the problems of mountaineering and to read his accounts of the first crossings of the Jungfraujoch and Eigerjoch is to capture something of the spirit of the age. He climbed mountains solely for fun and relaxation and, as a result, his writings make better reading than the dry academic accounts of those who sought to conceal their love of mountains and mountain climbing beneath the vestments of science. Indeed he amused himself at the expense of Professor Tyndall when he wrote, apropos of the first ascent of the Zinal Rothorn, ". . . the temperature was approximately (I had no thermometer) 212° (Fahrenheit) below freezing-point. As for ozone, if any existed in the atmosphere, it was a greater fool than I take it for."

Like all the pioneers, and indeed like most Englishmen of action, Stephen was mortally afraid of allowing his pen to stray into a sentimental morass. It was one thing to love mountains and to discover inspiration upon them but quite another to endeavour to define or interpret that love. Like a love letter read in a law court, it became vulgar, even immoral, when exposed to the public eye. From the beginnings of mountaineering it has been left to the poets who, alas, with one or two exceptions were all non-mountaineers, to attempt to reveal the beauty of high places. This is not to say that mountaineering has not produced good literature. That it appealed to men of academic distinction ensured that it should receive its due. A good criterion of the worth of any sport is the literature it produces and, measured against the quality of its narratives, mountaineering is easily first of all sports. The story was good and it was well told, but like the best champagne it was very dry. Its limitations were imposed by the sheer inability of ordinary men to translate into intelligible language the immemorial call of the hills. And so we must be content to discern the Golden Age through books such as *Peaks, Passes and Glaciers*, of which a later mountaineer wrote that it was "so inspiring a gospel of adventure and full, free life, that the call summoned to the hills an army of seekers after the promised gold." In this way was the mystic call of Nature, so long the preserve of a few writers and poets, manifested through a new sport to ordinary men.

TWO STAGES IN THE ASCENT OF MONT BLANC
Colour prints by George Baxter, 1804-1867

VIEW OF BREIT-LAUWINEN

Coloured aquatint by C. M. Descourtis after G. Wolf

THE FIGHT FOR THE MATTERHORN

ONE summer's day in 1860, a youth aged twenty tramped up the stony mule-track along the St. Nicholas Thal to Zermatt. His name was Edward Whymper and he was apprenticed to his father's business of wood-block engraving. Already he had shown considerable artistic talent and William Longman, of the well-known publishing house of that name, had commissioned him to visit the Alps and make a series of sketches for a forthcoming publication.

A mile from Zermatt he turned a corner and the soaring peak of the Matterhorn came suddenly into view. Strangely enough this youth, aflame as he already was with the zest for mountain climbing, was not impressed. In his diary he wrote, "Saw of course the Matterhorn repeatedly ; what precious stuff Ruskin has written about this, as well as about other things. When one has a fair view of the mountain as I had, it may be compared to a sugar-loaf set up on a table ; the sugar-loaf should have its head knocked on one side. Grand it is, but beautiful I think it is not."

At Zermatt he was warmly welcomed as a recruit for mountaineering by the climbers assembled there, Leslie Stephen, Walker, Hinchliff and others, and the last named offered to coach him on the Riffelberg, an offer that was gratefully accepted. On this, his first Alpine season, he attempted no high or difficult ascents but he did a prodigious amount of walking and crossed several passes of moderate altitude, on one of which he was deserted by his guide, a circumstance which prejudiced him against guides : he had yet to learn that the skilled Alpine guide was of an altogether different calibre to the peasant who escorted tourists over easy passes.

The following year he returned to the Alps and, accompanied by R. J. S. Macdonald and a Frenchman, Jean Reynaud, made the first English ascent of Mont Pelvoux in Dauphiny ; a climb which gained for him entry into the Alpine Club the same year. Having thus whetted his taste for mountain adventure he began to look for more ambitious projects. The two finest peaks then unclimbed were the Weisshorn and the Matterhorn and, after an unsuccessful attempt to climb Monte Viso and a visit to the Mont Cenis tunnel in the construction of which he was keenly interested, he made for Breuil on the Italian side of the Matterhorn. He arrived there a few days after Professor Tyndall had made an unsuccessful attempt on the mountain, having already succeeded with his guide J. J. Bennen in climbing the Weisshorn. Whymper accordingly decided to lay siege to the Matterhorn and, undeterred by its local reputation for inaccessibility, sought out and engaged a guide. The latter proved little more efficient than his guide of the previous summer and, when the first real difficulty was encountered at 12,650 feet, declined to go on. This reverse had no other effect on the tough young Englishman than to make him more than ever determined to climb the mountain, which he believed to be accessible over the broken Italian ridge, and in 1863 he returned to the attack accompanied by Macdonald and two Zermatt guides. The weather was bad and an icy storm enveloped them above the Col du Lion. It was Whymper's first experience of a hurricane in the High Alps. He wrote, "We clutched our hardest when we saw stones as big as a man's fist blow away horizontally into space. We dared not attempt to stand upright, and remained stationary on all fours, glued, as it were, to the rocks." It was too much for the faint-hearted guides and they refused to return for another attempt.

Whymper was undaunted. This second reverse merely brought out his granite qualities. He was more than ever determined to succeed. Thus far he had had bad luck with guides, but a new figure now came on the scene. Jean-Antoine Carrel, the "Old Soldier" of Breuil, believed like Whymper that the Matterhorn could be climbed. Furthermore, he was determined to make the first ascent for the honour of Breuil and of Italy. He and his brother had already attempted it and, as a result, he considered the mountain as "a kind of preserve." He now condescended to allow Whymper to engage him as his guide.

This time the party advanced beyond their previous highest point, to a height of 12,992 feet at the foot of a huge rock pinnacle in the ridge known as the Great Tower, some 240 feet beneath the point attained by the Carrels the previous year. But once again bad weather supervened and enforced a precipitate retreat.

Macdonald then had to return to England. Whymper, left to his own devices, sought to engage Carrel but the latter could not, or would not, accompany him. So he went alone. It was a risky business, but to climb the Matterhorn had now become an obsession. His boldness and skill were rewarded when he reached a height of 13,400 feet, only 1,400 feet from the summit, but on the descent he narrowly escaped total disaster. He had

PROFESSOR TYNDALL
Drawing by George Richmond, 1864

passed the difficulties when, on rounding a corner, he slipped and fell nearly 200 feet down a steep gully. He managed to stop himself on the brink of a precipice and scramble up to a safe place before fainting away from loss of blood.

Most men would have been content to let well alone. Not so Whymper. A few days later, having recovered from his wounds, he set out for the fifth time, accompanied by the Carrels and Luc Meynet, a little hunchback who had already acted as porter, but again a sudden storm enforced retreat after a height of 13,150 feet had been reached.

Once again the haughty Carrel refused to accompany him, so he set out on a sixth attempt accompanied only by the hunchback. He reached a point a little above his previous highest but the steepness of the rocks and the weakness of the party made retreat obligatory. He arrived back at Breuil only to find that Professor Tyndall had arrived with his guides for another attempt on the mountain. At first Tyndall invited Whymper to join his party, but a little later rescinded the invitation, apparently on the advice of his guide Bennen who probably regarded Whymper as an irresponsible young hot-head, a circumstance that led to a bitter dissension between Tyndall and Whymper. Thus Whymper had the mortification of seeing the party start off without him, but had the somewhat vicarious satisfaction of pouring coals of fire on Tyndall's head by loaning him his tent which had been left on the mountain. Long and earnestly and tormented, as he writes, "with envy and all uncharitableness," he watched the mountain next day. At one time there was a report of "men on the summit," but in the evening he saw the party returning. "There was no spring in their steps—they, too, were defeated."

Between his attempts on the Matterhorn, Whymper made many other fine ascents including the Ecrins and various cols in Dauphiny, ascents in the range of Mont Blanc with Adams Reilly, the first passage of the very difficult Col Dolent which ranks to-day as one of the stiffest ice climbs in the Alps, the first ascent of the Aiguille Verte and various ascents in the Zermatt district. During most of these climbs he was accompanied by Michel Croz of Chamonix and it was from him, and also from Christian Almer of Grindelwald, that he learned the worth of a great guide. For both these men were great ; Croz was a man of verve, fire and titanic energy ; Almer tempered dash with caution, a man of superlatively good judgment. It was an admirable combination. The pity of it is that the Matterhorn was not assaulted earlier by this formidable trio.

The drama of the Matterhorn had in it all the elements of a Greek tragedy. Frustration, disappointment, mischance, all contributed to the final denouement. In 1864, Whymper had to hurry back to England just after he had arrived at Zermatt with Adams Reilly, having traversed the difficult and dangerous Moming pass, when everything was set for an attempt on the Matterhorn. Whether or not this would have been made by the east face is not certain but, had this route been attempted by this strong and competent party, there is little doubt that success would have been gained.

The 1865 season was a good one. Whymper was now beginning to realise that the east face of the Matterhorn was easier than it looked. Yet Croz and Almer were against it. In the end it was agreed to attempt one further possibility before investigating it. This was a great gully leading to a point high on the Furggen ridge of the mountain. It was an absurd route and showers of falling stones sent the party back in hasty retreat. The guides

ZERMATT
Water colour by John Ruskin

were discouraged ; they believed the Matterhorn to be impossible ; but Whymper was still undaunted, and proposed that instead of descending to Breuil they should straight away attempt the east face. It was necessary to cross the Furggjoch in order to reach the Hörnli at the foot of the face, but the pass proved more difficult than usual. As they stood there undecided, snow began to fall and in response to the entreaties of his guides Whymper was forced to return to Breuil.

After this, he climbed on the range of Mont Blanc and in the course of eighteen days ascended more than 100,000 feet of mountain-sides, many of them previously untrodden, a *tour de force* which stands unique in the annals of mountaineering.

But the Matterhorn was ever a lodestone and soon he returned to it. Unfortunately, Croz was unable to accompany him, having arranged the previous winter (on not hearing from Whymper until it was too late) to climb with Birkbeck, whilst Almer, when he heard of yet another proposed attempt, declared emphatically, "Anything but the Matterhorn, dear sir ! Anything but the Matterhorn." Thus Whymper reluctantly dismissed him at Breuil together with his other guide, Biener, who was even more emphatic

21

in his detestation of the mountain, and sought to engage Carrel. The latter was against leaving his beloved Italian ridge and attempting the Swiss side and it was eventually agreed that, in the event of failure on the east face, the Italian ridge should be again attacked.

On the evening of July 8th, when Whymper had completed his preparations for the east face, a messenger arrived at Breuil to say that an Englishman was lying seriously ill at Valtournanche. It was a call Whymper was unable to refuse, and he at once hastened down the valley. On the way he met an Italian with his baggage, accompanied by the two Carrels. Whymper told J. A. Carrel to remain at Breuil, and reminded him of his promise to accompany him over the Théodule Pass the same night. Carrel replied by saying that he had been engaged by a "family of distinction" and was not free to work for Whymper after the 11th.

Having walked down to Châtillon to procure medicine for the sick man, Whymper returned to Breuil on the 10th. The weather was bad next day and he was forced to remain idle. On the morning of the 11th he learned to his consternation that a large party of mountaineers, including Carrel, had set off for the Matterhorn. The "family of distinction" had been none other than Signor Giordano, a geologist and mountaineer, who was acting on behalf of Signor Sella, another Italian mountaineer. Whymper was furious ; he had been "tricked and bamboozled." But all was not yet lost. If he could only get to Zermatt over the Théodule Pass he might be able to engage guides and still make his attempt on the east face. But how ? There were no guides or mules available to accompany him. At this point Lord Francis Douglas arrived with his guide, young Peter Taugwalder. He had already made a fine ascent of the Ober Gabelhorn by a new route and on the strength of this Whymper suggested that they should join forces in an attack on the east face. Douglas agreed, and the combined party hastily crossed the Théodule to Zermatt where they engaged old Peter Taugwalder, the father of their present guide ; and then there arrived at Zermatt the Rev. Charles Hudson, together with his protégé, D. R. Hadow, a youth of nineteen, and Michel Croz who had been engaged by Hudson when Birkbeck had fallen ill. They, too, were intent on attempting the Matterhorn and, as it seemed to Whymper undesirable that there should be two parties on the same route at the same time, he suggested an amalgamation. Hudson agreed, and in response to Whymper's inquiry as to the capabilities of Hadow, replied that he, Hadow, had done Mont Blanc in less time than most men. This was true, but anyone sound in wind and limb can climb Mont Blanc, whereas a rock peak like the Matterhorn is an entirely different proposition. Hadow was totally unfitted to be in the party, and his inclusion was the prime cause of the disaster that followed. A secondary, but by no means unimportant cause was the large size of the party. The blame for the catastrophe that followed must be apportioned equally between Whymper and Hudson.

The party left Zermatt on July 13th, and proceeded over the Hörnli to

THE SUMMIT OF THE MATTERHORN
Engraving by Edward Whymper from the *Ascent of the Matterhorn*, 1880

the foot of the east face. They bivouacked at a height of 11,000 feet and, after a comfortable night, commenced the ascent. To his astonishment, Whymper found the rocks much easier than he had anticipated. Indeed the face was a fraud, and places that had appeared utterly impracticable when viewed from the Riffel were so easy that no rope was necessary for the greater part of the way. Making rapid progress they reached the point where a vertical cliff bars further progress over the face. To avoid this they bore to the right over a shoulder on to the upper part of the north face. Here the climbing was considerably more difficult for the rocks were slabby. (Fixed ropes now assist the climber over this section.) Hadow needed continual assistance, but all went well and at length the slope eased off. Here Whymper, who had been in a fever of impatience throughout the ascent, in case he were forestalled by Carrel and his party, dashed ahead with Croz to the summit. The snow was untrodden. But there was another and equally high summit. Together with Croz he hastened there. Suddenly he saw the Italians, mere specks far down their ridge. They were retreating ; their attempt had failed. With shouts of triumph Whymper and Croz prized away boulders with their ice-axes and sent them hurtling down the precipice.

Whymper had won, but his triumph was shortlived. For an hour the party remained on the summit basking in the sun and enjoying the marvellous panorama. Then they tied on the rope ready for the descent. Here a fatal mistake occurred. There were three ropes. Two were strong and one weak. It was intended to fix the weak one to the rocks in order to facilitate the descent of the difficult section. Instead, although there was more than enough strong rope for the whole party, the weak rope was used between Lord Francis Douglas and old Peter Taugwalder. This was subsequently to lead to much acrimonious controversy and scandalous assertion. Even Whymper went so far as to suggest that the substitution was effected by old Peter out of self-interest, and the poor old man was virtually hounded out of his native village and forced to reside abroad. Yet the responsibility, if any, was not his but Whymper's and Hudson's, while Croz, as leading guide, should have overseen the roping. It is better to regard the whole affair as an oversight, carelessness arising out of the natural elation of success and the desire to be down and off the mountain as quickly as possible. In any event, there were now two weak links in the chain, Hadow and the rope. The combination proved fatal.

The party were on the slabs. They were going slowly, one by one, and moving with the utmost circumspection. It was particularly trying work for Hadow, and Croz, who was first man down (as most experienced guide he should have been last), was taking hold of his feet and placing them on the small holds. Croz was moving down a step himself, and had laid aside his ice-axe the better to assist Hadow, when suddenly the latter slipped. Croz was caught quite unprepared. Hadow's feet struck him in the small of the back and knocked him from his holds. The two men fell. Hudson who was next on the rope was unable to resist the shock and was pulled from his steps and Lord Francis Douglas was similarly dragged down. The remaining three, the Taugwalders and Whymper, when they heard Croz's startled exclamation braced themselves as well as they could. Old Peter was moderately well placed and hugged a rock with his arms. The strain came. They held, but the weak rope between Lord Francis Douglas and old Peter Taugwalder snapped in mid air. The four falling climbers were beyond aid. For a few seconds Whymper and his companions endured the terrible spectacle of seeing them sliding down the slabs, spreading out their arms in vain endeavours to save themselves. Then they disappeared and fell down the great precipices of the north face on to the Matterhorn glacier four thousand feet beneath.

THE GLACIER DES BOSSONS, CHAMONIX
Water colour by John ('Warwick') Smith, 1786

THE MER DE GLACE OR GLACIER DES BOIS

Right, the Pic du Dru; left, the Charmos; behind, the Aiguille du Géant and the Jorasses

The descent of the three survivors was a nightmare. The Taugwalders were utterly unnerved, and momently Whymper expected another accident. At length, however, they reached the shoulder and began the descent of the easier east face. Here they were benighted but after a wretched bivouac were able to reach Zermatt next day.

In this way ended the most momentous and dramatic chapter in mountaineering history. The repercussions were many. The Press united in denouncing mountaineering as an absurd, foolish and unjustifiable sport, and so general was the condemnation that Queen Victoria was moved to inquire whether it could not be stopped by law. In the opinion of one great Alpine historian, Captain J. P. Farrar, the accident held back the tide of mountaineering for half a generation of man. Be this as it may, the check was only temporary. Whymper never again undertook great pioneer climbs in the Alps, even if he did in the Andes, and it is doubtful whether he ever really recovered from the disaster and the disagreeable publicity that followed upon it. Yet mountaineering had come to stay and British climbers were to take part in many another great pioneer climb both in the Alps and elsewhere.

"Croz! Croz! Come Here!"
Engraving by Edward Whymper from *Scrambles Amongst the Alps*, 1871

25

UNDOUBTEDLY the Matterhorn disaster had grave effects on British mountaineering, yet, if during the years immediately following 1865 there were few recruits to the sport, the Alpine Club continued its activities undismayed by public criticism and ridicule ; in doing so it acted in the best traditions of British sport. In the years following upon it there were numerous ascents : Mont Collon, one of the Pennine giants, was climbed by G. E. Foster in 1867 and the highest point of the Grandes Jorasses on the range of Mont Blanc fell to Horace Walker in 1868, Whymper having already climbed the secondary summit in 1865.

The 'seventies saw not only a marked revival of mountaineering but the advent of one of the most indefatigable British climbers that has ever trodden a mountain. This was the Rev. W. A. B. Coolidge, who in the company of Miss Brevoort made many ascents, particularly in the wild Dauphiny region. Coolidge was animated not only by a love of mountaineering but was interested in its history, and became its leading historian as well as a writer of guide-books remarkable for the exactness and accuracy of their information. There can have been few more dogmatic and forceful clerics. It is said that he quarrelled with practically every member of the Alpine Club, and his quarrels more than once resulted in his resignation from the Club, for mountaineers take themselves, their sport, their opinions, and their veracity very seriously. His most famous quarrel was with Edward Whymper, whose account of a jump during the first traverse of the Ecrins in 1864 he questioned in the course of his obituary notice of Christian Almer, and the Alpine firmament vibrated to the thunder of the doughty and self-opinionated contestants. Coolidge's greatest ascent was that of the Meije in Dauphiny, one of the finest and most difficult peaks in the Alps. Others of his Dauphiny ascents included the Grande Ruine, the Pic Coolidge, Les Bans, and the southern Aiguille d'Arves. Coolidge survived well into the age of modern mountaineering and was well known as the "Lion of Grindelwald," at which place he resided for many years.

If the technique of snow and ice craft was scarcely capable of advancement, except in the study of snow and glacier conditions, rock climbing offered promise of ever increasing skill and daring. The greatest rock climb made during the Golden Age was undoubtedly that of Carrel's party, who succeeded in reaching the summit of the Matterhorn via the Italian ridge, and a most sensational traverse across the west face of the mountain by what is now known as Carrel's Gallerie, but it was not until the 'seventies that this specialised form of mountain craft took on a new lease of life. Among its exponents were Dr. Güssfeldt, who was without question the greatest Continental mountaineer of the day, de Castelnau and Duhamel, not to mention Coolidge who by his ascent of the Meije may almost be said to have inaugurated it.

THE GRANDES JORASSES AND THE DOIRE TORRENT, VAL FERRET
Engraving by Edward Whymper from *Scrambles Amongst the Alps*, 1871

An even more specialised form of rock climbing developed with the ascents of the granite slabs, cracks and chimneys of the Chamonix Aiguilles (needles) and the rough vertical precipices of the Dolomites. Some who read this will have visited Chamonix and ascended to the Montanvert. They will remember the clustered Gothic-like spires of the Aiguilles grouped before the serene snow dome of Mont Blanc, and in particular the terrific peak of the Dru. To the unitiated this last looks hopelessly impracticable, but its highest point was reached by Messrs. C. T. Dent and Hartley as long ago as 1878, an ascent that stimulated the equally difficult ascent of the second peak in 1879 by a Chamonix guide named Charlet. Thus was the fashion set for a new and even more exacting form of climbing.

27

The 'eighties and 'nineties might almost be described as the Silver Age of British mountaineering. They saw the ascent of the highest point of the tooth-like Aiguille du Géant by W. W. Graham, who was later to make some great pioneer ascents in the Himalayas to heights up to 24,000 feet, and the ascent of the Aiguille Blanche de Péteret, one of the buttressing peaks of Mont Blanc, perhaps the most formidable mountain in the Alps, by Sir H. S. King. But prince among rock climbers, and the prototype of the modern rock climber and mountaineer, was A. F. Mummery. It has been said that he was blackballed for the Alpine Club because of his guide-less climbing, and that when he sought election a second time Coolidge, who was not so conservative as some of his elderly confrères, quietly slipped some of the "no's" from the ballot box into the "aye's." Be this as it may, Mummery's example, and not least his fresh and joyous style of writing as exemplified in his classic *My Climbs in the Alps and Caucasus*, exercised a profound influence on mountaineering. If the old boiling-point thermometer and geological notebook excuse for mountain climbing still prevailed in certain quarters, Mummery killed it stone-dead. He climbed simply and solely for the fun of the thing. The thinnest, most elegant, most difficult of the Chamonix pinnacles were grist to his mill, and to his doughty guides Alexander Burgener and Venetz. The Aiguile des Grands Charmoz fell in 1880, and the following year saw him poised on the top block of the now world-famous Grépon, after the hardest rock climb that had ever been accomplished up cracks and slabs that even to-day scarcely constitute "an easy day for a lady" contrary to Mummery's own optimistic speculations, though ladies nowadays do far harder climbs than that. Mummery was not one ever meekly to follow behind guides, and in the company of his friends Professor Norman Collie, Geoffrey Hastings and W. C. Slingsby, who earned for himself a great name as the pioneer of Norwegian mountaineering, he made the first ascent of the Dent du Requin, another formidable needle on the range of Mont Blanc. He was, however, no mere rock gymnast as his attempt on the north ice wall of the Aiguille du Plan and the first crossing of the fearsome Col du Lion between the Matterhorn and the Tête du Lion testifies, for these are ice climbs of extreme severity, whilst the first ascent of the Matterhorn by the Zmutt ridge was first and foremost a great mountaineering achievement. It is a curious circumstance that of the early explorers of this last-mentioned route nearly all of them died violent deaths within a few years. Among them was Burgener, one of the strongest and finest guides the Alps have known, who was killed by an avalanche near the Bergli hut in the Bernese Oberland. It is probable that Mummery died in the same way. In 1895 he visited the Himalayas, accompanied by Professor Collie and the late Brigadier-General the Hon. C. G. Bruce, to attempt the ascent of the 26,660-foot peak of Nanga Parbat. After one determined attempt he set out with two Gurkha orderlies to cross a high glacier pass and if possible make another. He was never seen again,

THE PASS OF LLANBERIS, WALES
Engraving from John Ball's *Peaks, Passes and Glaciers*, 1859

and it is presumed that the party was overwhelmed by an ice avalanche. Perhaps the fairies believed to dwell there took him to themselves. The name Mummery still pervades mountaineering. Long after many famous names are forgotten simple natives will point upwards to the shining snows of Nanga Parbat and say, "There Mummery Sahib lies." Who could wish for a better epitaph or a grander resting place ?

Nanga Parbat has since been attempted by a German-American expedition and three German expeditions. Two met with disaster from storm and avalanche, and it would seem that it had little use for Hitler and the swastika. The mountain became a sort of preserve for Germans and it is well, therefore, to remember Mummery and his Gurkhas. When Mr. Eric Shipton and I proposed making an attempt I received indignant letters from Germany. It was, according to my correspondents, unsporting of us to try ; the mountain was Germany's. British mountaineers do not look on mountaineering in this way. If they have been the only ones to attempt Mount Everest it was because the Tibetan Government categorically refused permission for any but a British expedition. Perhaps with their Oriental insight and love of peace, as well as veneration for their holy mountains, they realised what an infiltration of Nazi gospellers would mean.

The growth of mountaineering has ever been animated by the desire to explore, the longing to tread where no human foot has trodden before. In its beginnings the quest was for new peaks, but when the peaks were climbed the pioneering instinct devolved into a search for new routes, a search that has perforce developed of recent years into attempts to master the all but impossible. Side by side with the later developments of Alpine mountaineering the technique of rock climbing, and even of snow and ice work on a limited scale, was developed on the British hills. This was all to the good.

It prepared men and women for the more difficult and complicated art of Alpine climbing. They learned self-reliance on the hills in all manner of weather, they gained an eye for mountain country and learned above all to climb rocks of extreme difficulty safely and confidently. There is no space here for the story of British rock climbing ; it is a history in itself. It is associated with many great names such as Mr. W. P. Haskett Smith, J. M. Archer Thompson, the Abraham brothers and Owen Glyn Jones who was killed on the Dent Blanche in 1899. To-day, climbing in Wales, the Lake District and Scotland, where Alpine conditions are to be found in late winter and spring, especially on the north face of Ben Nevis, and where climbs as fine and long as some of those on the Chamonix Aiguilles may be enjoyed on the gabbro of the Coolins in Skye, is a fine art, so much so that the rubber-shoes expert, accustomed to spend hours in negotiating a cliff of super severity, finds himself at a disadvantage when called upon to climb a great Alpine peak where speed over ground of moderate difficulty is the first essential. Then the British rocks afford those of limited means or too short a holiday for the Alps with the keenest form of concentrated enjoyment. Literature, as already indicated, has had much to do with the popularising of mountaineering. Several books have already been mentioned. There were many others, whilst in recent years a steady stream has developed into a spate.

If the Alps are now the "Playground of Europe" the Dominions still afford scope for the same pioneering instinct that distinguished the Golden Age of Alpine climbing. The great peaks of the Rockies, such as Mount Robson and Mount Assiniboine, the complicated ridges of the Selkirks, and the wild tangle of peaks of the Coast Range of British Columbia, have yielded up their secrets to Canadian, American and British mountaineers. In New Zealand, Mount Cook was first of all climbed and then traversed by a route that ranks in difficulty and interest with any of the greater climbs on the south side of Mont Blanc, and the New Zealand Alpine Club, like the Canadian Alpine Club, has been indefatigable in opening up one of the wildest and loveliest regions of the world. Yet, it is perhaps in the Himalayas that British mountaineering has attracted most attention of recent years ; this will be dealt with in the next chapter. The Golden Age of climbing and exploration will last longer here than in the Alps. It will not be ten years ; it may well extend over ten generations.

Finally, British mountaineers have introduced their sport to many other lands, to the Andes of South America where the names of Conway, Whymper and Fitzgerald will ever be remembered ; to Japan, where it has a huge following thanks to the enthusiasm of the late Rev. Walter Weston ; to the Caucasus of which men such as Freshfield, Mummery and Donkin were the pioneers ; to Norway where the late William Cecil Slingsby is recognised as the Father of Norwegian mountaineering ; and to many other odd corners of the earth.

A CAMP IN THE HIMALAYAS
Lithograph after a drawing by Capt. Sir E. P. Campbell, Bt.

THE HIMALAYAS: MOUNT EVEREST

AFTER the Alps, the story of Himalayan climbing is the most interest-ing and in many respects the most dramatic in the history of mountain-eering. When it is remembered how enormously mountaineering skill and technique has advanced of recent years and how, thanks to science and invention, equipment has improved, it must be a source of wonder to many that out of the fifty or sixty summits in the Himalayas exceeding 25,000 feet only two, Nanda Devi and Kamet, have so far been reached, whilst Mount Everest, Kangchenjunga, K.2, and Nanga Parbat remain inviolate despite the best endeavours of the pick of British, American, German, Austrian and French mountaineers. Yet to anyone who has climbed amidst these two thousand miles of mountains with their innumerable summits exceeding 20,000 feet, it is not difficult to understand. Many of the lesser peaks have been ascended, some of them fifty and more years ago, but above 25,000 feet new factors come into operation. Roughly, there are three main diffi-culties in high Himalayan climbing ; the difficulty of the mountain, and the Himalayas being geologically young are steeper than the more weathered Alps, the altitude, and the weather.

The first difficulty is purely technical, but it interacts with the second. A place that to surmount in the Alps merely requires a simple arm-pull may well prove impossible at 26,000 feet because of the lack of energy-giving oxygen. Men have reached 28,000 feet without any artificial aid. Therefore it is known that every summit bar, possibly, Everest, is physiologically accessible, and it is probable that Everest also can be reached. To a large extent the body adapts itself to the lack of oxygen at high altitudes, which adaptation is gained by the climber who climbs slowly, stage by stage. At the same time, above 21,000 to 23,000 feet a deterioration of physique takes place, leading to a rapid loss of weight and appetite, to sleeplessness and a reduction of physical and nervous stamina ; so that in the words of Mr. Eric Shipton a mountaineer high on Everest is like "a sick man climbing in a dream." The third difficulty, the weather, is the greatest difficulty of all, and in almost every case of failure on a great Himalayan peak, storm and blizzard, or an unusually early onset of the monsoon, has been primarily responsible.

High Himalayan mountaineering is therefore a most complex problem in which many different factors have to dovetail into one another like a jig-saw puzzle before success can be achieved.

As in the case of Alpine mountaineering the early visitors to the Himalayas were mostly travellers, geographers and scientists. In this connection names such as Godwin-Austen, the discoverer of K.2, the Schlagintweit brothers, Sir Joseph Hooker and Sir Francis Younghusband will be remembered.

Then came the explorer-mountaineer, Lord Conway, the Duke of the Abruzzi, the Bullock Workmans, General Bruce, W. W. Graham (who was, however, more of a mountaineer than anything else), Dr. E. Neve, Dr. A. M. Kellas, Dr. T. G. Longstaff, whose ascent of Trisul, 23,406 feet, in 1907, remained the highest for more than twenty years, D. W. Freshfield, and C. F. Meade. It was not until after the Great War that mountaineers began to devote their energies specifically to the ascent of one or other of the great peaks.

Climbing Everest or any other of the highest peaks of the Himalayas is a very different affair from climbing a peak in the Alps. The latter takes no longer than two or, at the most, three days ; the former may take several months, and is akin to a rush for the Pole in its concentrated hardships, difficulties, dangers and discomforts. Its motif is achievement, rather than pleasure, though there is always pleasure in achievement. To enjoy Himalayan mountaineering aesthetically one should keep below the 25,000-foot level and tackle peaks of moderate altitude where the fight is against the mountain rather than against your own incapacities in the thin, cold air at greater altitudes.

Everest stands on the frontiers of Nepal and Tibet, both countries normally closed to Europeans, and it was not until 1920 that the Dalai Lama, the ruler of Tibet, gave permission for British climbers to visit Mount Everest. The expedition that went next year was primarily a reconnaissance,

JUMNOTREE, THE SOURCE OF THE RIVER JUMNA
Drawn by J. B. Fraser and engraved by R. Havell & Son

and its principal climber, George Leigh-Mallory, discovered what appeared
to be a possible route up the mountain, and reached a height of 23,000 feet
on the North Col, which lies between Everest and the neighbouring North
Peak. Yet it would be foolish to limit an Everest party merely to climbers

THE MOUNT EVEREST EXPEDITION, 1938
Camp 6, showing the East Rongbuk Glacier

when so much valuable scientific work can be accomplished, and succeeding expeditions, with the exception of the 1938 expedition, tackled Everest with the knowledge that, even though they failed to climb the mountain, they would bring back valuable physiological, geological, topographical, botanical, zoological and ethnological data, in this way justifying the expenses of the expedition.

In 1922 Capt. G. I. Finch and Major Bruce reached a height of over 27,000 feet aided by oxygen apparatus, whilst another party, consisting of Mallory, Dr. T. H. Somervell and General E. F. Norton, got to nearly 27,000 feet without using oxygen apparatus. A little later the monsoon broke and the warmer airs and snowfalls which it brought rendered the slopes of the North Col so dangerous that when an attempt was made to re-open Camp Four an avalanche occurred and seven of the native porters were swept over an ice cliff and killed.

In 1924 a third expedition made a determined attempt to reach the summit. Terrible weather and temperatures more than 20° below zero Fahrenheit were experienced, and this, combined with the lack of oxygen, which is as much the fuel of the human body as petrol is of a motor car, drove the party down to the base camp. They returned, and eventually Norton and Somervell established a camp at 26,800 feet and from it made

THE MOUNT EVEREST EXPEDITION, 1938
Camp 6, showing the slabs and the North-East Ridge

an attempt on the summit. At 28,000 feet Somervell was unable to continue because of a frostbitten and congested throat due to rapid breathing in the intensely cold dry air. Norton struggled on alone for another hundred feet before exhaustion compelled him to retreat also. Had it not been for the terrible hammering they had already endured from the weather on the East Rongbuk glacier and the North Col it is probable that they would have succeeded.

A few days later Mallory and the youthful Andrew Irvine set out to make another attempt, this time using oxygen apparatus. N. E. Odell, who was splendidly acclimatised and should by virtue of his greater mountaineering experience have accompanied Mallory in place of the comparatively inexperienced Irvine, followed the party a day behind them to collect geological specimens. On the day they left the highest camp to make their attempt on the summit he saw them "going strong" along the broken crest of the northeast ridge. It was only a fragmentary glimpse between swirling mists and it was the last ever seen of them, for they failed to return. In Mallory, Everest lost its most formidable opponent and mountaineering one of its most brilliant figures. Of him Norton wrote, "It was the spirit of the man that made him the great mountaineer he was : a fire burnt in him and caused his willing spirit to rise superior to the weakness of the flesh." He was indeed "a knight 'sans peur et sans reproche' amongst mountaineers."

Not until 1933 was there another Everest expedition. This experienced terrible weather and was repeatedly driven back from the slopes of the North Col by blizzards ; then by even worse weather from Camp Five at 25,700 feet, where some of the porters were badly frostbitten. If the porters had thrown in their hand they could hardly have been blamed, but the Sherpas from the Sola Khombu valley in Nepal and the Bhotias from Tibet are much more than porters. They are adventurers ; they are astoundingly tough ; they are natural mountaineers capable of withstanding cold and hardship ; they are cheerful, brave, and intensely loyal. When the final chapter of Everest comes to be written their names and accomplishments deserve to be inscribed in letters of gold. But the porters were not only willing but anxious to return to the attack. "We will pitch a camp higher than any camp has been pitched before. Then it is up to the sahibs to finish the job." Such was their spirit. They did.

Camp Six was pitched at 27,400 feet, and from it two attempts were launched on the summit, firstly by P. Wyn Harris and Lawrence Wager, and secondly by Eric Shipton and myself. Both failed at 28,100 feet, the height reached by Norton in 1924. Once again the weather supervened and by covering the smooth outward-shelving slabs in powdery snow rendered the ascent impossible. During the course of their attempt Wyn Harris and Wager discovered an ice-axe which can only have belonged to either Mallory or Irvine. It is thought that one of them slipped. The other put down his axe the better to hold the rope in both hands and check the fall of

WEDGE PEAK
One of the peaks of the Kangchenjunga group

his sliding companion. He failed to do so and the ice-axe was left there, sole testimony of the disaster.

Since 1933 there have been two more attempts and one reconnaissance, but cruel luck dogged the footsteps of the climbers, for exceptionally early monsoons prevented them from getting as high as the 1924 or 1933 expeditions. The 1938 expedition struggled up to over 27,000 feet but found it impossible to tread the roof-like slabs leading towards the final pyramid owing to quantities of soft and unstable new snow.

That Everest can be climbed there is no doubt, and probably without the aid of oxygen apparatus which although ideal in theory has been found difficult to adapt practically to the steep and difficult work near the summit, owing to its weight, clumsiness and the limited amount of gas that can be carried by the climber. Turning to other aspects of Himalayan mountaineering, the small British expedition that I organised in 1931 was successful in climbing the first of the twenty-five-thousanders, Kamet, 25,443 feet. In 1936 another British expedition went one better by climbing Nanda Devi, 25,660 feet, the highest peak in British-administered territory, whilst it is interesting to note that a Polish expedition succeeded in climbing the lower but very difficult east peak of the same mountain in 1939. Meanwhile the Germans were busy in attempts on Kangchenjunga and Nanga Parbat. Those on Kangchenjunga were marked by exceptional skill under the leadership of Paul Bauer and were carried out with great energy and determination in the face of extreme technical difficulty. The same cannot be said of Nanga Parbat. It is obligatory on Himalayan climbers to safeguard their lines of communication so that in the event of bad weather the party can retreat to well-stocked camps. This the Germans failed to do and, instead of getting the two fittest climbers to the highest camp well supported from lower camps, as is the usual procedure on Everest, a large group of them collected there together with their porters. Then the weather broke. The tents, evidently of poor fabric, failed to withstand the tearing force of the wind, and they were forced to retreat in the storm. The retreat developed into one of the greatest catastrophes in mountaineering, and the great majority of the party died of cold, hunger and exposure. An even worse disaster occurred in 1937 when a party pitched a camp within range of ice avalanches and were overwhelmed in the night, sixteen Germans and porters perishing.

The foregoing sketches but briefly some of the major features of Himalayan mountaineering. Much other less spectacular but very good work has been done, and it cannot be too emphatically stated that the Himalayas afford the mountaineer of modest means with a splendid field for exploration and climbing together with one or other of the branches of science. There are innumerable peaks round about 20,000 feet of a difficulty sufficient to test the most skilful of Alpine-trained experts, and it is on such peaks that the sport of mountain climbing is best discovered in the Himalayas.

A PERSONAL ADVENTURE

I am now going to tell you about a personal experience which happened to me in Switzerland—in the Bernese Oberland. One day in July, 1925, a friend, Mr. J. H. B. Bell, and I left Grindelwald and walked up to the Strahlegg hut, one of the refuges built for climbers. We intended to climb the Schreckhorn, the most formidable peak in the district. Incidentally, Schreckhorn means Terror Peak; it is an appropriate name as I have good cause to remember. After a couple of nights at the hut we climbed the mountain over its difficult south-west ridge. The weather was perfect, so much so that we went on to traverse the neighbouring peak of the Lauteraarhorn. It was a longish day and took us nineteen hours. The Schreckhorn certainly failed to live up to its reputation then, and I remember with something more than ordinary pleasure our long scrambles over its rough firm rocks.

After that, Bell and I planned another climb, but in reconnoitring it Bell damaged his foot and we were unable to start off for it. Meanwhile, two other climbers, Messrs. A. Harrison and C. M. K. Douglas, had arrived at the Strahlegg hut intending to climb the Schreckhorn, and it occurred to me that they would enjoy the ascent over the south-west ridge, the route Bell and I had taken, much better than the ordinary easier route. So I asked them if they would care to join forces. They were agreeable ; thus for a second time I found myself setting off to climb the Schreckhorn.

Dawn was just breaking as we walked over the little Schreck glacier towards the mountain. It was a very queer dawn, one of the most extraordinary I have ever seen in the mountains. The sky overhead was clear but in the south great banks of oily clouds were piled up in heaven ; but they were a long way off and seemed powerless to harm us. What was queer about that dawn was its colour. The earth and the atmosphere were pervaded with a green tinge and when the sun rose it poured not its usual red glow on the mountain tops, but the same unearthly green, a green the colour of the light emitted by an X-ray tube. None of us had seen anything like it before and we didn't know what to make of it. However, the sky around remained clear and we saw no particular reason for abandoning the climb and returning to the hut. So we carried on, and presently the green colour vanished in the full flood of the risen sun and everything seemed to promise fair weather and an enjoyable scramble.

In order to reach the crest of the south-west ridge we had to climb a wide gully about twelve hundred feet high. It was not an easy job getting into the gully because the foot of it was defended by a *bergschrund*, which is simply a large crevasse separating the foot of a mountainside from the glacier at the base of it. Fortunately at one place there was a tongue of snow bridging the rift and we were able to crawl gingerly across one by one, each of us held by his two companions on the rope. Above the *bergschrund* was a steep ice slope. Up this we cut steps with our ice-axes and presently found ourselves well in the gully. Here the going was easier up slabby rocks and patches of well-frozen snow and we made rapid progress. At the same time it was not a place to take liberties with and I dare say would have seemed a horrible place to anyone who wasn't a mountaineer.

At seven o'clock we emerged from the gully on to the rocky crest of the south-west ridge, and had only to clamber along it to reach the summit, which was now full in view, another twelve hundred feet or so above us.

But before going on we stopped for a bite of breakfast. As we ate we had a good look at the weather. It was much the same as before. The sky overhead was clear and the sun was shining brightly whilst in the south the same oily masses of cloud were poised over the distant Rhône valley and the ranges of the Pennine Alps. There seemed no immediate prospect of it breaking, and even if it did we told ourselves that we would be over the summit and down the mountain by the ordinary way without trouble. So once more we decided to carry on. The south-west ridge of the Schreckhorn is very steep and sharp but it is also very firm, and made of a rough, reddish-coloured schistose. It was a sheer delight to climb. Here and there were difficult bits, vertical walls, over which we had to move one at a time, but for the most part we could climb all together. So engrossed were we with the climbing that we never gave another thought as to the weather, and in warm sunlight scrambled up and up towards the sharp summit of the mountain which every minute loomed nearer and nearer.

We were about five hundred feet from the top when, of a sudden, we heard a long-drawn peal of thunder. We paused and looked round. A few minutes before the north-west sky had been clear, but now it was choked by a great wall of inky black cloud. It was an extraordinary formation, clear-cut and level like the crest of an ocean roller, and it extended across the whole width of the sky in that direction. It did not take us more than a few moments to realise that this cloud was moving towards us and moving with amazing rapidity. Every second the thunder boomed louder and louder

THE VALLEY OF THE JUMNA SHOWING THE TWO GRAND PEAKS OF BUNDER PUNCH
Drawn by J. B. Fraser, engraved by R. Havell & Son, from Fraser's *Himalayas*, 1820

BEN NEVIS

Water colour by William Turner of Oxford

until its peals were merged into a continuous din. It was exactly as though some devastating artillery barrage was creeping in our direction.

Between us and the approaching storm stood the peak of the Eiger and we saw the clouds engulf it and vicious tongues of lightning stab and flicker all over it. There was no time to retreat ; we must find what shelter we could. In any event it was essential to get off the knife-like crest of the ridge on which we stood as it would soon be a target for the lightning.

It is often difficult or impossible to descend from the crest of an Alpine ridge, but luck was with us. Twenty feet lower was a ledge partially sheltered by an overhanging bulge of rock above. We were able to climb down to it and there we sat in a row with our legs dangling over the precipice. As it seemed to us that the steel heads of our ice-axes might attract the lightning we left the axes lying on a patch of snow near the crest of the ridge.

We had not long to wait for the storm. We heard the furious bombardment of the elements as they expended some of their fury on the Eiger. Then the sun suddenly disappeared behind a whirling smother of mist and the storm was upon us. The Schreckhorn is a sharp isolated peak and it received the full blast of the electrical energy locked up in the thunderclouds. There was a sudden blinding flash of mauve fire and a simultaneous explosion, not the crackle and roll one usually associates with a thunderstorm, but a sharp violent explosion like a bomb. Then came another flash and another and another. Then the heavens opened to release a deluge of hailstones, a curtain so dense that in a matter of seconds the mountain was white with racing cascades. Through the hail the lightning burst in blue flames and the mountain seemed to shake and shudder to the explosions of thunder. How near it was striking I cannot say, but it cannot have been more than a few yards distant because the thunder seemed simultaneous with the lightning. Suddenly there was a flame that seemed to scorch our very eyebrows and fill the air with darting streams of blue fire. There was a crack like a colossal whip, then a crash, and a mass of rock split off from the crest of the ridge by the lightning hurtled past us and plunged down the precipice. For a moment we wondered whether we were still alive, but we had little time to wonder about that or anything else for the flames and explosions were deafening and stunning in their frequency and force. I do remember, however, that in one brief lull Harrison remarked imperturbably, "Well, I came though the whole war in the Suicide Club (which as you may remember was the name given to the Machine Gun Corps) and was several times the only officer left alive, so we ought to get through this all right."

Meanwhile the hail had changed to snow and this fell so fast that the rocks were soon covered two or three inches deep. Things began to look pretty unpleasant, but just when we were wondering how we were going to get down again the storm suddenly eased off, the thunder and lightning ceased as though by magic, and the sun peered out. We clambered back to the ridge where to our relief we found our ice-axes uninjured ; more than once we had wondered whether they would have been destroyed by the lightning. The question now was whether to go on or go back. If we went on we should have to climb five hundred feet over snow-covered rocks but should get an easier route down. If we went back by the way we had come the going would certainly be difficult with so much new snow on the rocks. On the other hand, supposing another storm developed, to be caught on or near the top of the Schreckhorn was not to be thought of for a moment. We decided to retreat by the way we had come. It was a providential decision. Had we not made it I should not have lived to tell the story.

The slushy snow concealing the handholds and footholds made the climbing difficult and our descent correspondingly slow. We were not far from the point where we had to leave the ridge and descend the twelve-hundred-foot gully when again we heard the ominous and horrid booming of thunder. We made every effort to get off the crest of the ridge into the gully but quick as we were the storm was quicker still. As we reached the head of the gully and turned away from the ridge into it the storm was upon us like a tiger, an even worse storm than the first if that were possible, a hurricane of wind, hail and snow and appalling nerve-shattering lightning. The topmost part of the gully consisted of smooth rock slabs and now that these were covered in snow climbing was none too easy. Harrison and Douglas were below moving cautiously step by step whilst I was above them in the responsible post of last man down. I was a few feet below the crest of the ridge and was feeling a bit more confident now that I was not on that lightning-blasted crest. But something, Providence again if you like, made me decide to halt and put the rope round a projecting rock until my friends were in a safer position. I had only just done this when I received a tremendous blow on the head, just as though I had been sandbagged. At the same moment I have a dim recollection of blinding blue fire and a terrific concussion. For a second or two there was blackout, then I woke up to find myself off my holds and hanging on the rope. Had I not placed the rope round the projecting rock I must have fallen and pulled Harrison and Douglas with me to destruction. Amid the general inferno of wind, blizzard, and crashing thunder they were unaware of what had happened and were still moving down. I shouted to them, "I've been struck," and they paused. Then I made my way slowly and painfully down to them. I was trembling all over and it was only with the greatest difficulty that I could control my limbs.

Providence had not finished its intervention in our favour. We had to halt a few minutes to give me time to recover. A little later, a fall of rock, doubtless dislodged by lightning from higher up the mountain, fell into the gully a short distance beneath us and swept it from end to end. Had it not been for the delay due to my being struck by lightning we must have been right in its path and been wiped off the slate.

THE SCHRECKHORN FROM THE GRINDELWALD GLACIER
Sketch by E. T. Coleman from *Peaks, Passes and Glaciers*
Volume II, edited by E. S. Kennedy, 1862

But our troubles were by no means at an end ; indeed the worst was to come. The storm developed to a pitch of ferocity such as I have never experienced before or since in the Alps. The wind reached a hurricane. Worse still, the temperature fell and the slush and water that had melted during the brief interval of fine weather between the storms froze on the rocks in sheets of ice. It was a case of hacking away with our ice-axes and of groping with our hands for the holds. Our progress got slower and slower. Frequently we were unable to move at all, and for minutes at a time had to cling on as best we could while the blizzard raged at us, beating us with snow until our clothing and faces were sheeted with ice and we could barely see out of our eyes. I shall never forget the sound of the wind. The lightning was still striking the ridge to one side of the gully ; we could see its streams of fire, yet the wind rivalled the crash of the thunder. Sometimes its approaching gusts made a noise like an express train in a tunnel ; sometimes they tore up the gully with a terrible, tearing, rending sound, sometimes they burst upon us with a roar like thunder. So thick was the writhing, wind-tortured snow that frequently we could not see one another, and one man would step down on the head of another, whilst the rope became so encased in ice as to be almost unmanageable.

It could not go on. In four hours we had descended only about 700 feet, little more than half the gully. The wind and the cold were doing their work.

Our hands had lost feeling, our bodies were getting colder and colder. The fight could not go on much longer. Presently there would be collapse, a slip and—finish.

It was then that Providence came to our aid for the fourth time that day. The snow-clouds swept aside, the wind dropped. It was a miracle. Somebody said, "What about some chocolate ?" It had been impossible to eat before. Now it was possible ; that chocolate put life-giving warmth and energy into our bodies. The dead feeling left them and we were able to go on moving even if very slowly. The storm returned but not with the same force as before. We could keep on going. It took six hours to descend that twelve-hundred-foot gully but we did it at last. Our steps in the ice slope below had been blotted out by the blizzard, but we were able to cut a new staircase. We could not find the snow bridge over the crevasse but we found a place we could jump. So at last we reached the glacier, and our difficulties were over. There we shook hands ; we had not expected to get down ; it was a gesture of thankfulness. For my part I could not wish for two more stout-hearted companions than Harrison and Douglas.

We paused to gaze up at the snow-wreathed crags of the Schreckhorn and to listen to the wild orchestra of the storm still raging among them. Then, very tired, we trudged down to the longed-for warmth and shelter of the Strahlegg hut.

MODERN MOUNTAINEERING

B Y the end of the last century all the major peaks of the Alps had been climbed, many of them by several routes, and mountaineering in Europe was sharpening its skill in a search for more and more difficult routes. During the present century the search has become greatly intensified, so that it is now possible to say that climbing has reached the limit of human power and skill and that to overstep it merely entails the employment of extraneous aids. The most significant development has been the increase in guideless climbing. Here again it is interesting to note British mountaineers took the principal pioneering part. Some of the climbs of Hudson and Kennedy have already been mentioned. Then there was Girdlestone who wrote *The High Alps Without Guides*, the first volume on guideless climbing, which was however greeted with disapproval by his contemporaries of the Alpine Club who had come to regard the guide as a *sine qua non* of respectable mountaineering. But with the passing of the eclectic age and the popularising of mountaineering, guideless climbing became an inevitable and logical development of the sport, because not only did it make mountaineering possible for the would-be climber with limited funds but it catered for the independent and adventurous instinct of young men. The old days when the guide was no more certain than his employer that a peak could be climbed had passed ; routes were well known and the guides who climbed them did so almost to a time-table. To-day the craft of guiding is a rapidly dying business put out of action by its own superlative efficiency. The fact is that it is far, far better fun to climb without guides, and if guiding is to persist its principal functions can only be training those who want to learn the mountain craft and conducting tourists up fashionable peaks such as the Matterhorn and Mont Blanc. Failing such employment it is safe to say that guiding will be virtually extinct before another generation has passed.

The first fourteen years of the twentieth century were good years for British mountaineering. They saw such mountaineers as Messrs. Raeburn and Ling, Hope and Kirkpatrick, H. O. Jones, Captain Percy Farrar who represented all that was best in British mountaineering, Mr. R. L. G. Irving who incurred the censure of the Alpine Club by taking his pupils up mountains without guides, but whose justification was the production of George Mallory and several other fine mountaineers who added greatly to the credit of the sport. Then there was Mr. G. Winthrop Young (the present President of the Alpine Club), the doyen of modern British mountaineering, and the greatest of its poets, who by precept and example exercised a profound influence upon it.

Yet thus far, that is up to 1914, mountain craft progressed gracefully and rhythmically, reflecting as it were the settled and slowly progressive policies of the age. The Great War divided mountaineering into two distinct streams. It is indeed interesting, in view of the recent conflict, to examine briefly the development of the sport in this light.

The well-being of any great sport depends on the traditions of good sportsmanship established by generations of good sportsmen. Mountaineering is no exception. It has had its rivalries and jealousies, what sport has not ? but until the past twenty years it has been singularly free from any taint of nationalism. Mountaineers of all nations were concerned to climb for the fun of climbing, and even the fight for the Matterhorn hinged on personal rivalry and ambition, and Whymper's imputation that Carrel was anxious to climb the mountain for the honour of his native valley and of Italy was probably more of a dramatic touch than anything else. Of late years the cheap and sensational Press has made much of the Everest expeditions from a national standpoint, but the climbers themselves would be the first to refute a charge of nationalism ; they have tried to climb Everest simply because they wanted to climb it and for no other reason. After the last war, however, a different spirit began to manifest itself on the Continent. Germany had been beaten, and the Germans are a proud people ; it was necessary above all things that they should rehabilitate themselves in the eyes of the world. They must be not only good sportsmen but the *best* sportsmen, better than the sportsmen of any other nation. This infection, founded as it was on a sense of grievance and inferiority, manifested itself in every international sports gathering in which Germans took part ; it was particularly marked at the Olympic Games, it impinged with brutal force on the fair sport of ski-ing ; with the advent of Hitlerism it spread to mountaineering. I became first cognisant of it during the International Kangchenjunga Expedition of 1930 when every member was issued with a flag which he was expected to keep flying over his tent. It was the ambition of the Germans to plant their flags on the top of each mountain. The emblem issued to me was a Union Jack with the stripes the wrong way round, made in Germany. Running short of pocket handkerchiefs on one occasion I used it as a substitute to the horror of my German companions. Possibly, indeed, the alleged decay of democracy dates from this. It was this flag-waving inferiority complex, for it was nothing else, that led the Germans into their desperate assaults on jealously "preserved" mountains and into equally desperate assaults in the Alps on mountain-sides that no sane mountaineer with any responsibilities would have embarked upon. It led also to the new, and, in the opinion of British climbers, undesirable technique of scaling otherwise impossible rock faces by means of pitons (iron spikes). One may admire the courage of the performers but scarcely the spirit animating the performance. As in other field sports the merit of mountain climbing lies in the simple and direct contact of the sportsman with the terrain. It lies also in knowing where to draw the line. An ice-axe, nailed boots and crampons may be accounted necessary implements in the craft of mountaineering, but to hammer a way up precipices by means of scores of

IN THE GARHWAL HIMALAYAS, 1937
Camp at 20,000 feet on the Mana Peak

spikes and nails is outside the customs and traditions of the sport. The fisherman is not only concerned with the number of fish he catches; if he were he would employ dynamite. The Germans of the Third Reich preferred dynamite. Except in the increase of guideless climbing and the use of rubber shoes on the extremely difficult routes now undertaken on the British crags there is essentially no difference in the spirit in which climbs are now made by British mountaineers than that existing seventy-five years ago. It may be expedient to climb Mount Everest with oxygen apparatus, but speaking personally I would prefer to fail on that mountain without oxygen rather than to climb it with oxygen, for to my mind the whole charm of mountaineering lies in the employment of skill and energy with the minimum of artificial aid. It is the climbing, not the getting up that matters most in mountaineering.

It is to be hoped that from now on the sportsmen of the world will realise that it is the sport alone that counts and that future international contests will help to promote the best, not bring out the worst in men, for it is only thus that the sportsman can truthfully say, "it was worth while."